This book belongs
to chesslie Thomas
2012

TO

FROM

DATE

D0775771

Gene DeVaughn
Prattville, AL 36066
www.redlineministries.org

The quoted ideas expressed in this book (but not Scripture verses) are not, in all cases, exact quotations, as some have been edited for clarity and brevity. In all cases, the author has attempted to maintain the speaker's original intent. In some cases, quoted material for this book was obtained from secondary sources, primarily print media. While every effort was made to ensure the accuracy of these sources, the accuracy cannot be guaranteed. For additions, deletions, corrections, or clarifications in future editions of this text, please write Gene DeVaughn.

The Holman Christian Standard Bible™ (HCSB) Copyright © 1999, 2000, 2001 by Holman Bible Publishers. Used by permission.

The New American Standard Bible®, (NASB) Copyright © 1960, 1962, 1963, 1968, 1971, 1972, 1973, 1975, 1977, 1995 by The Lockman Foundation. Used by permission.

The Holy Bible, New International Version (NIV) Copyright © 1973, 1978, 1984, by International Bible Society. Used by permission of Zondervan Publishing House. All rights reserved.

Cover Design by Gene DeVaughn and Bart Dawson
Page Layout by Bart Dawson

ISBN 978-1-60587-132-5

Printed in the United States of America

UNSTOPPABLE

30 devos for TEEN GIRLS about God's unstoppable plan for your life!

UNSTOPPABLE

30 devos for TEEN GIRLS about God's unstoppable plan for your life!

STOP

TABLE OF CONTENTS

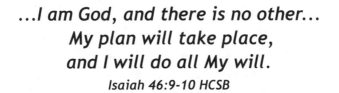

...I am God, and there is no other...
My plan will take place,
and I will do all My will.
Isaiah 46:9-10 HCSB

INTRODUCTION

Every girl loves a happy ending. Wouldn't it be nice if you always got the guy, the job, the home, the family and everyone lived happily ever-after? The reality is that life doesn't always work out that way. All of us will face trials in life. They're unstoppable! The question is: how will you deal with them when they come? God also says that His Word is unstoppable. It *will* accomplish what He desires. His Church also can't be stopped. Over the centuries people have tried to shut down and silence God's people, but all they did was cause the Church to spread!

So over the next 30 days, let's dive in to God's Word and learn about His unstoppable plan for *your* life!

TRIED AND TRUE

Blessed be the God and Father of our Lord Jesus Christ, the Father of mercies and the God of all comfort. He comforts us in all our affliction, so that we may be able to comfort those who are in any kind of affliction, through the comfort we ourselves receive from God. For as the sufferings of Christ overflow to us, so our comfort overflows through Christ. If we are afflicted, it is for your comfort and salvation; if we are comforted, it is for your comfort, which is experienced in the endurance of the same sufferings that we suffer. And our hope for you is firm, because we know that as you share in the sufferings, so you will share in the comfort. For we don't want you to be unaware, brothers, of our affliction that took place in the province of Asia: we were completely overwhelmed—beyond our strength—so that we even despaired of life. However, we personally had a death sentence within ourselves so that we would not trust in ourselves, but in God who raises the dead. He has delivered us from such a terrible death, and He will deliver us; we have placed our hope in Him that He will deliver us again. And you can join in helping with prayer for us, so that thanks may be given by many on our behalf for the gift that came to us through the prayers of many. For our boast is this: the testimony of our conscience that we have conducted ourselves in the world, and especially toward you, with God-given sincerity and purity, not by fleshly wisdom but by God's grace.

2 Corinthians 1:3-12 HCSB

TODAY'S UNSTOPPABLE TRUTH

Trials help you experience God in a deeper way.

HERE'S A QUESTION YOU MAY HAVE ASKED BEFORE:

If God is good, why would He allow painful trials in a believer's life?

Over the next few days we'll answer this question by taking a closer look at the passage above. There are benefits of trials if we keep our eyes on God and *not* on our circumstances! Paul said:

Blessed be the God and Father of our Lord Jesus Christ, the Father of mercies and the God of all comfort. ***He comforts us in all our affliction…*** *(vv. 3–4a)*

Trials help you experience God in a deeper way, but it sure doesn't seem like it when you're in the middle of it! We usually feel distant from, and abandoned by, God. He knows what you're going through and He has a purpose for the trials in your life.

Paul said the Lord was the "God of all comfort." The word "comfort" means *a calling to one's aid*. Christ can comfort you in your trials because

He has literally "been there and done that." Look how the writer of Hebrews puts it:

In bringing many sons to glory, it was fitting that God, for whom and through whom everything exists, should make the author of their salvation perfect through suffering.

Hebrews 2:10 NIV

Two chapters later, he goes on to say:

For we do not have a high priest who is unable to sympathize with our weaknesses, but One who has been tested in every way as we are, yet without sin. Therefore let us approach the throne of grace with boldness, so that we may receive mercy and find grace to help us at the proper time.

Hebrews 4:15-16 HCSB

Christ sympathizes with our *temptations* and *trials* because of what He went through during His time on earth. The word "sympathize" (vv. 15) means *to be affected with the same feeling as another.* He was tried and tempted in every way, yet without sin. He knows what you're feeling, therefore, He can *perfectly* relate to, and comfort you in, your painful situations!

If you're going through a trial right now; don't pull away from God, "approach the throne of grace." He's the "God of all comfort" from whom you can "receive mercy." And remember, your trial won't last forever. God will bring you through it "at the proper time."

Do you see God as "the Father of mercies," or do you have a twisted view of Him?

Maybe it's hard for you to "approach" your earthly dad with your problems, but remember that God is always there and ready to help...if you ask!

MORE TRUTH

God is the only one who can make the valley of trouble a door of hope.

Catherine Marshall

MEMORY VERSE

Blessed be the God and Father
of our Lord Jesus Christ, the Father of mercies
and the God of all comfort.
He comforts us in all our affliction…
2 Corinthians 1:3–4a HCSB

DO I LOOK OK?

*[God] comforts us in all our affliction so that
we will be able to comfort those who are in any
affliction with the comfort with which
we ourselves are comforted by God.*
2 Corinthians 1:4b

TODAY'S UNSTOPPABLE TRUTH

Your trials bring opportunities for you to extend
a helping hand to someone else…
if you look for them!

If you will keep your eyes on God and *not* on your situation, He will give you a ministry to others who are going through the same thing you've gone through.

My wife and I tried to have children for 10 years with no success. We found out that we could help people dealing with infertility because we had gone through it! We finally adopted our daughter Reagan and three years later (on our anniversary) we found out we were pregnant with our second daughter Gracen. Even though we now have children, we're still seeing the benefits of the pain we went through.

I recently got a call from a friend who found out she may never be able to get pregnant. She said, "I just wanted to talk to you and Lesley [my wife] because you know *exactly* what my husband and I are going through."

Trials are not fun at the time, but they can teach us a lot about God and ourselves. Rather than becoming bitter at God for allowing us to go through some tough situations, we should look for opportunities to share our stories about God's faithfulness *even* in bad times!

Will you allow trials to make you *bitter* or *better?*

Is there someone in your class, on the team or at work who is going through a hard time right now?

Have you ever taken the time to notice?

Will you take the time to "comfort" them?

MORE TRUTH ABOUT TOUGH TIMES

Recently I've been learning that life comes down
to this: God is in everything. Regardless of what
difficulties I am experiencing at the moment, or
what things aren't as I would like them to be,
I look at the circumstances and say,
"Lord, what are you trying to teach me?"

Catherine Marshall

In order to realize the worth of the anchor,
we need to feel the stress of the storm.

Corrie ten Boom

Measure the size of the obstacles against
the size of God.

Beth Moore

MEMORY VERSE

*Everyone should look out
not only for his own interests,
but also for the interests of others.*
Philippians 2:4 HCSB

CLOSER THAN EVER

…you are sharers of our sufferings,
so also you are sharers of our comfort.
2 Corinthians 1:7b NASB

TODAY'S UNSTOPPABLE TRUTH

Trials allow a special connection
to exist among believers.

You may be thinking, "What would Paul know about my trials," and how would that help me relate to him? Paul experienced more than his share of painful situations:

Five times I received from the Jews 40 lashes minus one. Three times I was beaten with rods. Once I was stoned. Three times I was shipwrecked. I have spent a night and a day in the depths of the sea.

On frequent journeys, I faced dangers from rivers, dangers from robbers, dangers from my own people, dangers from the Gentiles, dangers in the city, dangers in the open country, dangers on the sea, and dangers among false brothers; labor and hardship, many sleepless nights, hunger and thirst, often without food, cold, and lacking clothing. Not to mention other things, there is the daily pressure on me: my care for all the churches. Who is weak, and I am not weak? Who is made to stumble, and I do not burn with indignation? If boasting is necessary, I will boast about my weaknesses.

2 Corinthians 11:24–30 HCSB

Paul was persecuted for his faith. *(vv. 24-26)*
"Five times I received…thirty-nine lashes…I was beaten with rods…I was stoned… and… I have been…in dangers…among false brethren."

He had physical trials in his life. *(vv. 27)* *"I have been in…hardship, through many sleepless nights… often without food, in cold and exposure."*

He had emotional trials in his life. *(vv. 28-29)* *"Apart from such external things, there is the daily pressure on me…for all the churches…Who is led into sin without my intense concern?"*

Paul's trials didn't cause him to doubt or become bitter at God. *(vv. 31)* *"…God…is blessed forever…"*

Even in all that pain, Paul never stopped praising God! All this came from a guy who was either a widower or had never been married:

I say to the unmarried and to widows: **It is good for them if they remain as I am.** *But if they do not have self-control, they should marry, for it is better to marry than to burn with desire…Now I am saying this for your own benefit, not to put a restraint on you, but because of what is proper, and* **so that you may be devoted to the Lord without distraction.**

1 Corinthians 7:8-9; 35 HCSB

Whether Paul had experienced the death of his wife, or if he had never been married (we don't know which); he turned that trial into an opportunity to serve God!

MORE TRUTH

Suffering is never for nothing.
It is that you and I might be conformed
to the image of Christ.
Elisabeth Elliot

MEMORY VERSE

So we must not get tired of doing good,
for we will reap at the proper time
if we don't give up.
Galatians 6:9 HCSB

TRUST ISSUES

For we don't want you to be unaware, brothers,
of our affliction that took place in the province of
Asia: we were completely overwhelmed—beyond
our strength—so that we even despaired of
life. However, we personally had a death sentence
within ourselves **so that we would not trust in**
ourselves, but in God *who raises the dead.*
2 Corinthians 1:8-9 HCSB

TODAY'S UNSTOPPABLE TRUTH

Trials will show you exactly whom
or what you are trusting in.

Paul said he despaired for his own life because his situation was so bad! The word "despaired" literally means *no passage.*

Paul was thinking, "There's no way out, I'm dead!" God's purpose was to take away any chance of Paul falling back on his own intellectual, physical or emotional ability. Trials will show you *exactly* where your trust lies.

One of my favorite characters in the Bible is a little known guy named Mephibosheth. This guy knew about trials even at an early age! He was Jonathon's son and King Saul's grandson, and he shows us how to correctly respond in tough times:

Saul's son Jonathan had a son whose feet were crippled. He was five years old when the report about Saul and Jonathan came from Jezreel. His nurse picked him up and fled, but as she was hurrying to flee, he fell and became lame. His name was Mephibosheth.

2 Samuel 4:4 HCSB

When he was five years old his dad was murdered and his grandfather committed suicide. *(1 Samuel 31:2, 4) "The Philistines...killed Jonathan...So Saul took his sword and fell on it."*

He was handicapped for life because of someone else's carelessness. *"...His nurse took him up and fled. And...in her hurry to flee, he fell and became lame."*

He was defined by his handicap. *(He was known as the crippled guy [4:4; 9:3, 13]). "Jonathan...had a son crippled in his feet."*

Even with all of this happening to him; he trusted God and said, *"What right do I have...that I should complain...?" (2 Samuel 19:28b)*

You can't control the circumstances placed in your life, but you can control your attitude toward life.

MORE TRUTH

Don't let circumstances distress you.
Rather, look for the will of God for your life
to be revealed in and through
those circumstances.

Billy Graham

MEMORY VERSE

*Should we accept only good from God
and not adversity?*
Job 2:10b HCSB

I'M EXPECTING

*[God] delivered us from so great a peril of death,
and will deliver us, He on whom
we have set our hope.*
2 Corinthians 1:10a NASB

TODAY'S UNSTOPPABLE TRUTH

Trials help you to expect more from God.

Because God has proven Himself faithful in the past, we can praise and trust Him in the tough times ahead. David said:

I will praise the LORD at all times; His praise will always be on my lips.

Psalm 34:1 HCSB

He went on to say:

The righteous cry out, and the LORD hears, and delivers them from all their troubles. The LORD is near the brokenhearted; He saves those crushed in spirit. Many adversities come to the one who is righteous, but the LORD delivers him from them all.

Psalm 34:17-19 HCSB

Did you catch what David said?

When you cry, the Lord hears you. (vv. 17)

When you're troubled, He delivers you. (vv. 17)

When you're brokenhearted, He is near you. (vv. 18)

When you're crushed in spirit, He saves you. (vv. 18)

When you have many afflictions, He delivers you from them all!
(vv. 19)

Paul had learned to expect great things from God because of what he had gone through in his life. Twice in that verse, Paul said, "He *will* deliver us." His trials strengthened his faith so much that he later wrote:

Now to Him who is able to do above and beyond all that we ask or think—according to the power that works in you—to Him be glory in the church and in Christ Jesus to all generations, forever and ever. Amen.

Ephesians 3:20–21 HCSB

MORE TRUTH ABOUT GOD'S FAITHFULNESS

God will never let you sink under your
circumstances. He always provides a safety net
and His love always encircles.

Barbara Johnson

Our future may look fearfully intimidating, yet
we can look up to the Engineer of the Universe,
confident that nothing escapes His attention or
slips out of the control of those strong hands.

Elisabeth Elliot

The Lord God of heaven and earth, the
Almighty Creator of all things, He who holds
the universe in His hand as though it were a very
little thing, He is your Shepherd, and He has
charged Himself with the care and keeping of
you, as a shepherd is charged with the care
and keeping of his sheep.

Hannah Whitall Smith

MEMORY VERSE

I will praise the LORD at all times;
His praise will always be on my lips.
Psalm 34:1 HCSB

ALL EYES ON YOU

For our proud confidence is this: the testimony
*of our conscience, that **in holiness and godly***
***sincerity**, not in fleshly wisdom but in the grace of*
*God, **we have conducted ourselves in the world**,*
and especially toward you.
2 Corinthians 1:12 NASB

TODAY'S UNSTOPPABLE TRUTH

Trials expose your faith to the world.

Lost people watch us closely as we go through tough situations. They want to see if our faith in God is real. As God gives you opportunities to share about your own trials, remember to always take them to God's Word for guidance.

Here's a passage you can share that helps us keep trials in the right perspective:

For the Lord will not reject us forever. Even if He causes suffering, He will show compassion according to His abundant, faithful love. For He does not enjoy bringing affliction or suffering on mankind.

Lamentations 3:31–33 HCSB

Remember that trials are only temporary. *(vv. 31)* "*...the Lord will not reject us forever.*"

Even if it lasts your whole life, that's nothing compared to spending all eternity knowing you were faithful to God!

When God brings a trial in your life, His presence comes with it. *(vv. 32a)* "…*He will show compassion…*"

Just because you go through trials, doesn't mean that God doesn't love you. *(vv. 32b)* "…*according to His abundant, faithful love.*"

Your situation doesn't determine God's love for you, nor should it determine your love for Him!

It's not that God enjoys watching you go through trials; He has a purpose for them. *(vv. 33)* "*For He does not enjoy bringing affliction or suffering on mankind.*"

MORE TRUTH

Often the trials we mourn are really gateways
into the good things we long for.
Hannah Whitall Smith

MEMORY VERSE

For our proud confidence is this:
the testimony of our conscience,
that in holiness and godly sincerity…
we have conducted ourselves in the world…
2 Corinthians 1:12 NASB

YOU COMPLETE ME

Consider it a great joy, my brothers,
whenever you experience various trials,
knowing that the testing of your faith produces
endurance. But endurance must do
its complete work, so that you may be mature
and complete, lacking nothing.
James 1:2–4 HCSB

TODAY'S UNSTOPPABLE TRUTH

God has a specific purpose for every trial
you go through.

There's a certain amount of maturity that only comes through suffering. It's not fun, but it's necessary. It makes you stronger as a Christian, and James said we're not "complete" without it. It's like the tree that *only* becomes well rooted as it goes through storms! Paul said it this way:

And not only that, but we also rejoice in our afflictions, because we know that affliction produces endurance, endurance produces proven character, and proven character produces hope.

Romans 5:3-4 HCSB

Trials "prove" what you're made of! So the next time God takes you through a painful situation, open His Word again to Psalm 34 and let it be the calm in the middle of the storm:

The righteous cry out, and the LORD hears, and delivers them from all their troubles. The LORD is near the brokenhearted; He saves those crushed in spirit. Many adversities come to the one who is righteous, but the LORD delivers him from them all.

Psalm 34:17-19 HCSB

MORE TRUTH

Look upon your chastening as God's chariots
sent to carry your soul into the high places of
spiritual achievement.

Hannah Whitall Smith

MEMORY VERSE

*Many adversities come to the one
who is righteous,
but the LORD delivers him from them all.*

Psalm 34:19 HCSB

YOU SAID IT

A centurion's slave, who was highly valued by him, was sick and about to die. When the centurion heard about Jesus, he sent some Jewish elders to Him, requesting Him to come and save the life of his slave. When they reached Jesus, they pleaded with Him earnestly, saying, "He is worthy for You to grant this, because he loves our nation and has built us a synagogue." Jesus went with them, and when He was not far from the house, the centurion sent friends to tell Him, "Lord, don't trouble Yourself, since I am not worthy to have You come under my roof. That is why I didn't even consider myself worthy to come to You. But say the word, and my servant will be cured. For I too am a man placed under authority, having soldiers under my command. I say to this one, 'Go!' and he goes; and to another, 'Come!' and he comes; and to my slave, 'Do this!' and he does it." Jesus heard this and was amazed at him, and turning to the crowd following Him, He

45

said, "I tell you, I have not found so great a faith even in Israel!" When those who had been sent returned to the house, they found the slave in good health.

Luke 7:2-10 HCSB

TODAY'S UNSTOPPABLE TRUTH

God's Word is unstoppable whether we believe it or not. He says,
"My word…will not return to Me empty, without accomplishing what I desire, and without succeeding in the matter for which I sent it." (Isaiah 55:11)

The question we should be asking is, "How do I allow God's unstoppable Word to impact my life for His glory and my good?" We find the answer to that question in the passage you just read about a centurion (Roman soldier) who had an encounter with Jesus.

Over the next few days we'll see what we can learn from this guy. First of all, he understood that God's Word was unstoppable and it humbled him:

Humility causes you to realize you're not better than others. *(vv. 2) "…a slave…was highly regarded by him…"*

True humility will win the respect of others. *(vv. 3-4) "…Jewish elders…came to Jesus…saying, 'He is worthy for You to grant this to him…'"*

True humility puts others before your self. *(vv. 6-7)* "*...the centurion sent friends, saying to Him, 'Lord, do not trouble Yourself further, for I am not worthy for You to come under my roof...'*"

[If a Jewish person, like Jesus] entered a Gentile's house, [he] was [considered unclean] (Jn 18:28). The centurion, undoubtedly familiar with this law, felt unworthy of having Jesus inconvenienced for his sake (MacArthur).

When a believer lives a life of humility, God's unstoppable Word has the most impact for His glory and for the believer's own good! So what's the flipside of that? Here are a couple of examples of how an arrogant, self-centered life doesn't pay:

Example #1: In A.D. 303, Roman emperor Diocletian issued an edict to destroy scripture and those who held to it. Ironically, 25 years later, Roman emperor Constantine issued an edict ordering 50 copies of scripture prepared at the government's expense!

Example #2: Voltaire, the noted Frenchman who died in 1778, predicted that in 100 years from his time, "Christianity would be swept from existence." However, 50 years after his death, the Geneva Bible Society used his house and press to produce stacks of Bibles! Many have tried to burn it, ban it and outlaw it [but God's Word is unstoppable!]. *(The New Evidence that Demands a Verdict, Josh McDowell, pg. 10)*

MEMORY VERSE

My word…will not return to Me empty,
without accomplishing what I desire,
and without succeeding in the matter
for which I sent it.
Isaiah 55:11 NASB

WHAT'S THE WORD?

But say the word, and my servant will be cured. For I too am a man placed under authority, having soldiers under my command. I say to this one, "Go!" and he goes; and to another, "Come!" and he comes; and to my slave, "Do this!" and he does it.
Luke 7:7b-8 HCSB

TODAY'S UNSTOPPABLE TRUTH

God's Word has the most impact on your life when you accept it as the final authority.

The centurion simply took Christ at His Word. *(vv. 7) "...say the word, and my servant will be cured."*

Is Christ (and His Word) the absolute authority over your life? Take His Word over a family member, a best friend, someone you're dating, a college professor or *anyone* else!

Paul said this makes God's Word unstoppable in your life:

...this is why we constantly thank God, because when you received the message about God that you heard from us, you welcomed it not as a human message, but as it truly is the message of God, which also works effectively in you believers.

1 Thessalonians 2:13 HCSB

The centurion understood that he wasn't the final authority in his own life. *(vv. 8) "For I also am a man placed under authority..."*

"Authority" means *liberty of doing as one pleases*. Rather than thinking he was the boss of his own life, he was willing to obey his earthly authorities (Romans 13:1-7) and God's Word as his *ultimate* authority.

MORE TRUTH

Every experience God gives us,
every person he brings into our lives,
is the perfect preparation for the future
that only he can see.

Corrie ten Boom

MEMORY VERSE

…you welcomed it not as a human message,
but as it truly is the message of God,
which also works effectively in you believers.
1 Thessalonians 2:13 HCSB

I TOLD YOU SO

Jesus heard this and was amazed at him,
and turning to the crowd following Him, He said,
"I tell you, I have not found so great a faith even in
Israel!" When those who had been sent returned
to the house, they found the slave in good health.
Luke 7:9-10 HCSB

TODAY'S UNSTOPPABLE TRUTH

God's Word has the most impact on your life
when you acknowledge its reliability.

The centurion believed that God's Word was completely reliable! Look at the promises Jesus made about His Word:

For I assure you: Until heaven and earth pass away, not the smallest letter or one stroke of a letter will pass from the law until all things are accomplished.

Matthew 5:18 HCSB

Heaven and earth will pass away, but My words will never pass away.

Matthew 24:35 HCSB

Do you believe the Bible is completely reliable? Jesus said it will always be reliable, down to the smallest letter! Will you take Him at His Word? God also promised in the Old Testament that His Word is reliable and unstoppable:

Remember what happened long ago, for I am God, and there is no other; [I am] God, and no one is like Me. I declare the end from the beginning, and from long ago what is not yet done, saying: My plan will take place, and I will do all My will. I call a bird of prey from the east, a man for My purpose from a far country. Yes, I have spoken; so I will also bring it about. I have planned it; I will also do it.

Isaiah 46:9-11 HCSB

His Word can't be stopped because He is above all things. *(vv. 9) "…I am God, and there is no other; I am God, and there is no one like Me."*

His Word can't be stopped because it was planned from the beginning. *(vv. 10a) "Declaring the end from the beginning, and from ancient times things which have not been done…"*

His Word can't be stopped because it accomplishes His perfect will. *(vv. 10b-11) "…My purpose will be established, and I will accomplish all My good pleasure…Truly I have spoken; truly I will bring it to pass. I have planned it, surely I will do it."*

MORE TRUTH ABOUT GOD'S WORD

Weave the unveiling fabric of God's Word
through your heart and mind. It will hold strong,
even if the rest of life unravels.

Gigi Graham Tchividjian

There is no way to draw closer to God unless
you are in the Word of God every day.
It's your compass. Your guide.
You can't get where you need to go without it.

Stormie Omartian

Walking in faith brings you to the Word of God.
There you will be healed, cleansed, fed,
nurtured, equipped, and matured.

Kay Arthur

Words fail to express my love for this holy Book,
my gratitude for its author, for His love and
goodness. How shall I thank him for it?

Lottie Moon

MEMORY VERSE

For I assure you: Until heaven and earth
pass away, not the smallest letter
or one stroke of a letter
will pass from the law
until all things are accomplished.
Matthew 5:18 HCSB

IT'S AS GOOD AS DONE

Seek the LORD while He may be found; call to Him while He is near. Let the wicked one abandon his way, and the sinful one his thoughts; let him return to the LORD, so He may have compassion on him, and to our God, for He will freely forgive. "For My thoughts are not your thoughts, and your ways are not My ways." This is the LORD's declaration. "For as heaven is higher than earth, so My ways are higher than your ways, and My thoughts than your thoughts.

For just as rain and snow fall from heaven, and do not return there without saturating the earth, and making it germinate and sprout, and providing seed to sow and food to eat, so My word that comes from My mouth will not return to Me empty, but it will accomplish what I please, and will prosper in what I send it to do."

Isaiah 55:6-11 HCSB

TODAY'S UNSTOPPABLE TRUTH

God's Word will always accomplish
what He desires.

God emphatically said that His Word is unstoppable. In this one passage we see everything we've learned over the last few days:

It all begins with an attitude of humility. *(vv. 6-7)* *"Seek the* L<small>ORD</small> *while He may be found; call upon Him while He is near. Let the wicked forsake his way and the unrighteous man his thoughts; and let him return to the* L<small>ORD</small>*, and He will have compassion on him, and to our God, for He will abundantly pardon."*

Accept God and His Word as the absolute authority in your life. *(vv. 8)* *"For My thoughts are not your thoughts, nor are your ways My ways, declares the LORD. For as the heavens are higher than the earth, so are My ways higher than your ways and My thoughts than your thoughts."*

Acknowledge that His Word is completely reliable. *(vv. 11)* *"So will My word be which goes forth from My mouth; it will not return to Me empty, without accomplishing what I desire, and without succeeding in the matter for which I sent it."*

MEMORY VERSE

*For My thoughts are not your thoughts,
nor are your ways My ways,
declares the* LORD. *For as the heavens
are higher than the earth,
so are My ways higher than your ways
and My thoughts than your thoughts.*
Isaiah 55:8 HCSB

THERE'S NO STOPPING ME NOW!

I will build My church; and the forces of Hades will not overpower it.
Matthew16:18b HCSB

TODAY'S UNSTOPPABLE TRUTH

The world tries to stop the Church because we represent God's Son.

Jesus left no doubt that His Church is unstoppable when He said, *"...I will build My church; and the forces of Hades will not overpower it."* *(Matthew16:18b HCSB)*

However there will always be those who would love to shut down the influence of Christians all over the world.

Jesus went on to say:

Blessed are those who are persecuted for righteousness, because the kingdom of heaven is theirs. Blessed are you when they insult you and persecute you and falsely say every kind of evil against you because of Me. Be glad and rejoice, because your reward is great in heaven. For that is how they persecuted the prophets who were before you.

Matthew 5:10-12 HCSB

So here are the two big questions: Why does the world try so hard to silence Christians, and how could we possibly be "blessed" by being persecuted? Over the next few days we'll look at a passage where Jesus gives us the answers to those questions:

"If the world hates you, understand that it hated Me before it hated you. If you were of the world, the world would love you as its own. However, because you are not of the world, but I have chosen you out of it, the world hates you. Remember the word I spoke to you: 'A slave is not greater than his master.' If they persecuted Me, they will also persecute you."

John 15:18-20 HCSB

Persecution happens when you are different from the world. *(vv. 19)* *"If you were of the world, the world would love its own…but I chose you out of the world, because of this the world hates you."*

But they will do all these things to you on account of My name, because they don't know the One who sent Me. If I had not come and spoken to them, they would not have sin. Now they have no excuse for their sin. The one who hates Me also hates My Father. If I had not done the works among them that no one else has done, they would not have sin. Now they have seen and hated both Me and My Father. But this happened so that the statement written in their law might be fulfilled: They hated Me for no reason.

John 15:21-25 HCSB

If you're a believer who truly desires to live for God; you *will* face persecution:

In fact, all those who want to live a godly life in Christ Jesus will be persecuted.

2 Timothy 3:12 HCSB

Remember that persecution is really directed at Christ, not you. *(vv. 21)* *"But all these things they will do to you for My name's sake…"*

Christians are hated because we remind the world that God and His judgment are both a reality, but our *response* to their persecution can also remind them of God's grace! This happened with Paul and his friend Silas as they shared the Gospel while in prison.

We'll pick up with their story tomorrow, and then come back to our main passage here in John 15.

MORE TRUTH ABOUT PERSECUTION

Only believe, don't fear. Our Master, Jesus, always
watches over us, and no matter what
the persecution, Jesus will surely overcome it.

Lottie Moon

Fear lurks in the shadows of every area of life.
The future may look very threatening.
Jesus says, "Stop being afraid. Trust me!"

Charles Swindoll

MEMORY VERSE

*In fact, all those who want to live a godly life
in Christ Jesus will be persecuted.*
2 Timothy 3:12 HCSB

LOOK HOW SHE GLOWS

Then the mob joined in the attack against them, and the chief magistrates stripped off their clothes and ordered them to be beaten with rods. After they had inflicted many blows on them, they threw them in jail, ordering the jailer to keep them securely guarded. Receiving such an order, he put them into the inner prison and secured their feet in the stocks. About midnight Paul and Silas were praying and singing hymns to God, and the prisoners were listening to them. Suddenly there was such a violent earthquake that the foundations of the jail were shaken, and immediately all the doors were opened, and everyone's chains came loose. When the jailer woke up and saw the doors of the prison open, he drew his sword and was going to kill himself, since he thought the prisoners had escaped. But Paul called out in a loud voice, "Don't harm yourself, because all of us are here!" Then the jailer called for lights, rushed in, and fell down trembling before Paul and Silas. Then he escorted them out and said, "Sirs, what must I do to be saved?"

Acts 16:22-30 HCSB

TODAY'S UNSTOPPABLE TRUTH

It is in times of darkness
that the light of a Christian witness
shines brightest.

A godly response to persecution is to trust and praise God anyway. *(vv. 25a)* "*…about midnight Paul and Silas were praying and singing hymns of praise to God…*"

[They were stripped, beaten and put] "in stocks." This…was designed to produce painful cramping so the prisoner's legs were spread as far apart as possible (MacArthur). They were suffering for doing what was right, but they praised God rather than becoming bitter at Him!

A godly response to persecution will catch the attention of lost people. *(vv. 25b)* "*…the prisoners were listening to them.*"

The word "listening" means *to listen with pleasure,* as if listening to beautiful music. It is in times of darkness that the light of a Christian witness shines brightest. *(Nelson's New Illustrated Bible Commentary)*

A godly response to persecution is to care about those who persecute you more than your own comfort. *(vv. 27–28)* *"...the jailer...was about to kill himself...But Paul cried out...saying, 'Do not harm yourself, for we are all here!'"*

Paul and Silas stayed and risked going back to prison in order to save this guy's life.

Jesus prayed for the ones who nailed Him to the Cross (Luke 23:34), and Paul even said that he would take the punishment of hell for his fellow Jews if it were possible (Romans 9:3) (MacArthur). He would set aside his comfort in this life so others could be saved!

God can use your godly response to persecution in drawing people to Himself. *(vv. 29–30)* *"... trembling with fear [the jailer] fell down before Paul and Silas, and said, 'What must I do to be saved?'"*

MORE TRUTH

We must meet our disappointments,
our persecutions, our malicious enemies,
our provoking friends, our trials and temptations
of every sort, with an attitude of surrender and
trust. We must spread our wings and "mount up"
to the "heavenly places in Christ" above
them all, where they will lose their power
to harm or distress us.

Hannah Whitall Smith

MEMORY VERSE

*Do not repay anyone evil for evil.
Be careful to do what is right in the eyes
of everybody.*

Romans 12:17 NIV

LEAVE IT TO GOD

Up to the present hour we are both hungry and thirsty; we are poorly clothed, roughly treated, homeless; we labor, working with our own hands. When we are reviled, we bless; when we are persecuted, we endure it; when we are slandered, we entreat. We are, even now, like the world's garbage, like the filth of all things.

1 Corinthians 4:11–13 HCSB

TODAY'S UNSTOPPABLE TRUTH

There should be a sharp contrast in what
the world throws at us
and how we respond as Christians.

Yesterday we learned from Paul and Silas how to respond when we're being persecuted for our faith. Paul's entire ministry was an example of how to correctly respond to persecution:

Up to the present hour we are both hungry and thirsty; we are poorly clothed, roughly treated, homeless; we labor, working with our own hands. When we are reviled, we bless; when we are persecuted, we endure it; when we are slandered, we entreat. We are, even now, like the world's garbage, like the filth of all things.

1 Corinthians 4:11–13 HCSB

Notice the contrasts between what the world does and how we should respond:

"When we are reviled" *(means to vilify)*
"we bless" *(to speak well of and ask God to bless).*

"When we are persecuted" *(means to press)*
"we endure" *(to hold up under the pressure).*

"When we are slandered" *(means an evil report)*
"we entreat" *(striving to appease).*

Keep in mind though; some people will never be "appeased":

Bless those who persecute you; bless and do not curse. Rejoice with those who rejoice; weep with those who weep. Be in agreement with one another. Do not be proud; instead, associate with the humble. Do not be wise in your own estimation. Do not repay anyone evil for evil. Try to do what is honorable in everyone's eyes. **If possible, on your part, live at peace with everyone.** *Friends, do not avenge yourselves; instead, leave room for His wrath. For it is written: Vengeance belongs to Me; I will repay, says the Lord. But If your enemy is hungry, feed him. If he is thirsty, give him something to drink. For in so doing you will be heaping fiery coals on his head. Do not be conquered by evil, but conquer evil with good.*

Romans 12:14-21 HCSB

MEMORY VERSE

Do not be conquered by evil,
but conquer evil with good.
Romans 12:21 HCSB

THAT REMINDS ME

"If I had not come and spoken to them, they would not have sin. Now they have no excuse for their sin. The one who hates Me also hates My Father. If I had not done the works among them that no one else has done, they would not have sin. Now they have seen and hated both Me and My Father. But this happened so that the statement written in their law might be fulfilled: They hated Me for no reason. When the Counselor comes, the One I will send to you from the Father— the Spirit of truth who proceeds from the Father—He will testify about Me. You also will testify, because you have been with Me from the beginning. I have told you these things to keep you from stumbling."

John 15:22–16:1 HCSB

TODAY'S UNSTOPPABLE TRUTH

The world tries to stop the Church because
we remind them of their own sin.

**When you share God's Word with someone;
they no longer have an excuse.** *(vv. 22b)* "...*now
they have no excuse for their sin.*"

**Persecution will come even when you do nothing
to provoke it.** *(vv. 25)* "...*They hated Me for no
reason.*"

**God will help you speak His truth even in times
of persecution.** *(vv. 26-27)* "*When the Helper
comes, whom I will send to you...He will testify about
Me, and you will testify also...*"

**God has told us exactly what will happen so we
wont be surprised and begin to doubt.** *(vv. 16:1)*
"*These things I have spoken to you so that you may be
kept from stumbling.*"

MORE TRUTH

We are in a continual battle with the spiritual
forces of evil, but we will triumph when
we yield to God's leading and call on
His powerful presence in prayer.

Shirley Dobson

Where God's ministers are most successful,
there the powers of darkness marshal
their forces for the conflict.

Lottie Moon

MEMORY VERSE

*This is the verdict: Light has come
into the world, but men loved darkness
instead of light
because their deeds were evil.*

John 3:19 NIV

ARE YOU BLIND?

They will ban you from the synagogues.
In fact, a time is coming when anyone who kills you
will think he is offering service to God.
They will do these things because they
haven't known the Father or Me.
John 16:2-3 HCSB

TODAY'S UNSTOPPABLE TRUTH

The world tries to stop the Church because they
don't realize they're blinded by Satan.

This is why you see extremists blowing people up in the name of "God." They're sincere in what they're doing, but they're sincerely wrong! Satan has deceived them into believing a lie:

But if, in fact, our gospel is veiled, it is veiled to those who are perishing. Regarding them: the god of this age has blinded the minds of the unbelievers so they cannot see the light of the gospel of the glory of Christ, who is the image of God.

2 Corinthians 4:3-4 HCSB

Regardless of what people say or do to believers; the bottom line is that we *will* be victorious!

Who can separate us from the love of Christ? Can affliction or anguish or persecution or famine or nakedness or danger or sword? As it is written:

Because of You we are being put to death all day long; we are counted as sheep to be slaughtered. No, in all these things we are more than victorious through Him who loved us.

Romans 8:35-37 HCSB

Paul could say these things with confidence because he had been on both sides of persecution:

Saul [Paul's name before he was saved], *however, was ravaging the church, and he would enter house after house, drag off men and women, and put them in prison. So those who were scattered went on their way proclaiming the message of good news.*

Acts 8:3–4 HCSB

The more he tried to stop the Church, the more it spread. The Apostle Paul was a living example that the Church *cannot* be shut up or shut down. It's unstoppable!

MEMORY VERSE

*But if, in fact, our gospel is veiled,
it is veiled to those who are perishing.*
2 Corinthians 4:3 HCSB

IN THE END

*...it is appointed for men to die once
and after this comes judgment.*
Hebrews 9:27 HCSB

TODAY'S UNSTOPPABLE TRUTH

The resurrection and judgment of the unsaved
at the end of the Millennium
(thousand year reign of Christ) will be
a Day that changes everything forever.

Hebrews 9:27 says, "...*it is appointed for men to die once and after this comes judgment.*" It's not hard for people to believe that we're going to die because we see it happen all the time. However, most people either don't believe, or they just ignore, the fact that God's judgment will follow death. Physical death we can see, but spiritual death we can't see in this life...but Christ allowed the Apostle John to see it for us.

The Bible calls it "the great white throne" judgment:

"*Then I saw a great white throne and One seated on it. Earth and heaven fled from His presence, and no place was found for them. I also saw the dead, the great and the small, standing before the throne, and books were opened. Another book was opened, which is the book of life, and the dead were judged according to their works by what was written in the books. Then the sea gave up its dead, and Death and Hades gave up their dead; all were judged according to their works. Death and Hades were thrown into the lake of fire. This is the second death, the lake of fire. And anyone not found written in the book of life was thrown into the lake of fire."*

Revelation 20:11-15 HCSB

Over the next few days, we'll look closely at this passage and see what happens to an unbeliever when they die and stand before God at the Great White Throne Judgment.

This is the Day that earth and space will cease to exist. *(vv. 11) "Then I saw a great white throne and One seated on it. Earth and heaven fled from His presence, and no place was found for them."*

John said that the "earth and heaven fled away."

"heaven" means *sky*. He's talking about the entire physical universe.

"fled away" means *to vanish*.

God is going to destroy every part of the world as we know it because it's tainted by sin. Peter describes how it will happen:

But by the same word the present heavens and earth are held in store for fire, being kept until the day of judgment and destruction of ungodly men. Dear friends, don't let this one thing escape you: with the Lord one day is like 1,000 years, and 1,000 years like one day. The Lord does not delay His promise, as some understand delay, but is patient with you, not wanting any to perish, but all to come to repentance. But the Day of the Lord will come like a thief; on that day the heavens will pass away with a loud noise, the elements will burn and be dissolved, and the earth and the works on it will be disclosed.

2 Peter 3:7–10 HCSB

Even in God's judgment, you can see His mercy. *(vv. 9) "The Lord…is patient toward you, not wishing for any to perish but for all to come to repentance."*

"The heavens will pass away with a loud noise" The [word] "loud noise" [means] a whistling or crackling sound as objects [are] being consumed by flames. God will incinerate the universe, probably in an atomic reaction that disintegrates all matter as we know it (MacArthur).

It's one thing to hear the burning sound of a campfire, or even a big house fire, but imagine the sound of the entire universe being incinerated!

"The elements will be destroyed with intense heat." Peter means that the atoms, neutrons, protons, and electrons are all going to disintegrate (v. 11).

"The earth and its works." The whole...earth in its present form, with its entire universe will be consumed (MacArthur).

MEMORY VERSE

…it is appointed for men to die once
and after this comes judgment.
Hebrews 9:27 NASB

WHAT WERE YOU THINKING?

I also saw the dead, the great and the small,
standing before the throne, and books were opened.
Another book was opened, which is the book of life,
and the dead were judged according to their works by
what was written in the books. Then the sea gave up
its dead, and Death and Hades gave up their dead;
all were judged according to their works.
Revelation 20:12-13 HCSB

TODAY'S UNSTOPPABLE TRUTH

God knows our every thought.

Before God destroys the earth, the bodies of every unsaved person from all ages will rise from their graves (whether in the ground or sea). Their spirits are brought out of "Hades" (*hell*) to be re-joined with their bodies and instantly transformed into their supernatural bodies that can withstand their final destination, which is the "lake of fire" (we'll talk about that in a moment).

The "Book of Life" is opened to prove they are not saved because their names are not written in it. Other "books" are opened which record God's perfect knowledge of their every word, thought and action. These "deeds" will determine the degree of punishment each person will receive for all eternity. Does God really know us that intimately? Look what the Bible says in the following passages:

God knows your every thought:

For nothing is concealed that won't be revealed, and nothing hidden that won't be made known and come to light.

Luke 8:17 HCSB

The LORD knows man's thoughts; they are meaningless.

Psalm 94:11 HCSB

Knowing their works and their thoughts, I have come to gather all nations and languages; they will come and see My glory.

Isaiah 66:18 HCSB

MORE TRUTH

The things we think are the things that feed
our souls. If we think on pure and lovely things,
we shall grow pure and lovely like them;
and the converse is equally true.

Hannah Whitall Smith

As we have by faith said no to sin,
so we should by faith say yes to God
and set our minds on things above,
where Christ is seated in the heavenlies.

Vonette Bright

MEMORY VERSE

*Knowing their works and their thoughts,
I have come to gather all
nations and languages;
they will come and see My glory.*
Isaiah 66:18 HCSB

I HEAR YOU LOUD AND CLEAR

Either make the tree good and its fruit good, or make the tree bad and its fruit bad; for a tree is known by its fruit. Brood of vipers! How can you speak good things when you are evil? **For the mouth speaks from the overflow of the heart. A good man produces good things from his storeroom of good, and an evil man produces evil things from his storeroom of evil.** *I tell you that on the day of judgment people will have to account for every careless word they speak. For by your words you will be acquitted, and by your words you will be condemned.*

Matthew 12:33–37 HCSB

TODAY'S UNSTOPPABLE TRUTH

If you listen carefully to someone's words,
you can hear their heart loud and clear.

God will use people's words to judge them because they show what is truly in their heart (vv. 34b-35).

One of my youth Sunday School teachers recently saw a conversation one of her students was having on Facebook. The teacher was shocked by the language this girl was using because she seemed like such a committed Christian at church, but her words were showing what was really in her heart.

Like I said, if you listen carefully to someone's words, you can hear their heart loud and clear!

MEMORY VERSE

A good man produces good things
from his storeroom of good,
and an evil man produces evil things
from his storeroom of evil.
Matthew 12:35 HCSB

CAUGHT IN THE ACT

*One of his servants said, "No one, my lord the king.
Elisha, the prophet in Israel, tells the king of Israel
even the words you speak in your bedroom."*
2 Kings 6:12 HCSB

TODAY'S UNSTOPPABLE TRUTH

God knows our every action.

In the Old Testament, when the king of Aram would try to kill the Israelites, God would tell the prophet Elisha *exactly* what was going to happen and he would warn God's people. Aram's king thought there was a spy giving away his plans, but look what his servant told him:

One of his servants said, "No one, my lord the king. Elisha, the prophet in Israel, tells the king of Israel even the words you speak in your bedroom."

2 Kings 6:12 HCSB

The king's servant reminded him that God knows even our *private* thoughts, words and actions!

It's frightening to think that God knows us so well. Most people hope that if they just avoid thinking about the judgment to come, it will somehow go away. Paul met a governor named Felix who did this:

After some days, when Felix came with his wife Drusilla, who was Jewish, he sent for Paul and listened to him on the subject of faith in Christ Jesus. Now as he spoke about righteousness, self-control, and the judgment to come, Felix became afraid and replied, "Leave for now, but when I find time I'll call for you."

Acts 24:24–25 HCSB

He liked hearing about the love of Christ until he came to the part about repentance and the Day of Judgment. Then he gave a common response when he said, "I'll worry about this later *if* I find time."

Do you make time for God each day?

Do you like the fact that God sees *everything* you do?

MORE TRUTH

I am grateful that when even
a single sparrow falls the ground,
God knows—and understands.

Ruth Bell Graham

MEMORY VERSE

*Nothing in all creation is hidden from
God's sight. Everything is uncovered
and laid bare before the eyes of him
to whom we must give account.*

Hebrews 4:13 NIV

THEN WHAT?

Death and Hades were thrown into the lake of fire.
This is the second death, the lake of fire.
And anyone not found written in the book of life
was thrown into the lake of fire.
Revelation 20:11-15 HCSB

TODAY'S UNSTOPPABLE TRUTH

For those who have genuinely surrendered
their lives to Christ, the afterlife
is not something to be feared.

The first death is our physical death, and everyone will experience it. Remember the verse we started with which said, "*...it is appointed for men to die once and after this comes judgment.*" (Hebrews 9:27)

The unsaved will die the "second death" also. *(vv. 14) "This is the second death, the lake of fire."*

We will all die a physical death, but those who die unsaved will die a spiritual death also, meaning they will spend all eternity separated from Christ in torment.

However, let me remind you of God's mercy that was mentioned right in the middle of the passage we read earlier on God's judgment:

*The Lord does not delay His promise, as some understand delay, but is patient with you, **not wanting any to perish**, but all to come to repentance.*

2 Peter 3:9 HCSB

As a matter of fact, we need to read the rest of the passage that we began with in Hebrews:

And just as it is appointed for people to die once—and after this, judgment—so also the Messiah, having been offered once to bear the sins of many, will appear a second time, not to bear sin, but **to bring salvation to those who are waiting for Him.**

Hebrews 9:27-28 HCSB

For those who have genuinely surrendered their lives to Christ; the afterlife is not something to be feared.

We do not want you to be uninformed, brothers, concerning those who are asleep, so that you will not grieve like the rest, who have no hope. Since we believe that Jesus died and rose again, in the same way God will bring with Him those who have fallen asleep through Jesus. For we say this to you by a revelation from the Lord: We who are still alive at the Lord's coming will certainly have no advantage over those who have fallen asleep. For the Lord Himself will descend from heaven with a shout, with the archangel's voice, and with the trumpet of God, and the dead in Christ will rise first. Then we who are still alive will be caught up together with them in the clouds to meet the Lord in the air; and so we will always be with the Lord. Therefore encourage one another with these words.

1 Thessalonians 4:13-18 HCSB

Death is unstoppable. What happens to you after death can be decided right now. Ask Him to forgive your sins and make you a new person. Surrender your heart and life to Christ who defeated both death *and* hell!

MORE TRUTH

Your choice to either receive or reject
the Lord Jesus Christ will determine
where you spend eternity.
Anne Graham Lotz

Let us see the victorious Jesus, the conqueror of
the tomb, the one who defied death.
And let us be reminded that we, too,
will be granted the same victory.
Max Lucado

MEMORY VERSE

*Precious in the sight of the LORD
is the death of his saints.*
Psalm 116:15 NIV

THE "WONDER" OF HEAVEN

Be glad and rejoice,
because your reward is great in heaven.
Matthew 5:12 HCSB

TODAY'S UNSTOPPABLE TRUTH

One of the worst things about hell
may be knowing what you *could* have had!

True Christians don't have to wonder where they will spend eternity, but most of us do wonder what heaven will be like for us. Over the next three days, we'll look at eight questions that are commonly asked about heaven, and we'll let God Himself tell us what it's *really* going to be like.

Will we miss things here on earth?

For I will create new heaven and a new earth; **the past events will not be remembered or come to mind.**

Isaiah 65:17 HCSB

Speaking of former things, God said in Jeremiah 3:16, *"...in those days...it will not come to mind, nor will they remember it, nor will they miss it..."*

Will we recognize each other in heaven?

After six days Jesus took Peter, James, and his brother John, and led them up on a high mountain by themselves. He was transformed in front of them, and His face shone like the sun. Even His clothes became as white as the light. Suddenly, Moses and Elijah appeared to them, talking with Him. Then Peter said to Jesus, "Lord, it's good for us to be here! If You want, I will make three tabernacles here: one for You, one for Moses, and one for Elijah."

Matthew 17:1–4 HCSB

We can't say this definitively, but it seems that Peter knew who Moses and Elijah were even though he had never met them.

If our loved ones are in hell, won't that spoil heaven?

When the rich man in Luke 16 died and went to hell, the Bible says that he could see what he was missing in heaven; but there's no mention of Lazarus being aware of him in hell:

"There was a rich man who would dress in purple and fine linen, feasting lavishly every day. But a poor man named Lazarus, covered with sores, was left at his gate. He longed to be filled with what fell from the rich man's table, but instead the dogs would come and lick his sores. One day the poor man died and was carried away by the angels to Abraham's side. The rich man also died and was buried. And being in torment in Hades, he looked up and saw Abraham a long way off, with Lazarus at his side. 'Father Abraham!' he called out, 'Have mercy on me and send Lazarus to dip the tip of his finger in water and cool my tongue, because I am in agony in this flame!' 'Son,' Abraham said, 'remember that during your life you received your good

things, just as Lazarus received bad things, but now he is comforted here, while you are in agony. Besides all this, a great chasm has been fixed between us and you, so that those who want to pass over from here to you cannot; neither can those from there cross over to us."

Luke 16:19-26 HCSB

One of the worst things about hell may be knowing what you could have had!

MEMORY VERSE

*...No eye has seen, no ear has heard,
no mind has conceived what God
has prepared for those who love him.*
1 Corinthians 2:9 NIV

THE "WONDER" OF HEAVEN
(CONTINUED)

*Then be glad and rejoice forever in what
I am creating… The sound of weeping and crying
will no longer be heard in her.*
Isaiah 65:18-19 HCSB

TODAY'S UNSTOPPABLE TRUTH

Jesus carried our sin on the Cross to give us
eternal life, but ultimately He will
take away *all* grief and sorrow when He
brings us home with Him.

Yesterday we began answering the question: *If our loved ones are in hell, won't that spoil heaven?* Let's continue with that question and more.

The following passages let us know that we won't have the sadness of knowing our loved ones are in hell:

*He will wipe away every tear from their eyes. Death will exist no longer; **grief, crying, and pain will exist no longer, because the previous things have passed away.***

Revelation 21:4 HCSB

*Then **be glad and rejoice forever** in what I am creating...**The sound of weeping and crying will no longer be heard** in her.*

Isaiah 65:18-19 HCSB

He was despised and rejected by men, a man of suffering who knew what sickness was. He was like one people turned away from; He was despised, and we didn't value Him. Yet He Himself bore our sicknesses, and He carried our pains...

Isaiah 53:3-4 HCSB

Will we become angels in heaven?

People often say that a child, or loved one, who dies is now "my guardian angel."

Praise Him, all His angels; praise Him, all His hosts...Let them praise the name of the LORD, for He commanded, and they were created.

Psalm 148:2, 5 HCSB

Angels were created by God, and they are altogether separate from humans.

Where were you when I laid the earth's foundation? Tell me, if you understand. Who marked off its dimensions? Surely you know! Who stretched a measuring line across it? On what were its footings set, or who laid its cornerstone—while the morning stars sang together and **all the angels shouted for joy?**

Job 38:4-7 NASB

The Bible doesn't say exactly when they were created, but according to the passage we just read, it was before the creation of the earth *and people*.

Saying someone has become a guardian angel is just as wrong as standing over a loved one's grave, who never surrendered his life to Christ, and saying "He's in a better place."

MEMORY VERSE

Praise Him, all His angels;
praise Him, all His hosts…
Let them praise the name of the L ORD,
for He commanded, and they were created."
Psalm 148:2, 5 HCSB

THE "WONDER" OF HEAVEN
(CONTINUED)

*For I am persuaded that neither death nor life,
nor angels nor rulers, nor things present, nor things
to come, nor powers, nor height, nor depth, nor any
other created thing will have the power to separate us
from the love of God that is in Christ Jesus our Lord!*
Romans 8:38-39 HCSB

TODAY'S UNSTOPPABLE TRUTH

God will ultimately destroy all wickedness that
causes us to take our "eyes" off of Christ.

Will we ever be tempted to turn our backs on Christ in heaven?

No because believers will get an incredible new body at the resurrection:

"*So it is with the resurrection of the dead: Sown in corruption, raised in incorruption; sown in dishonor, raised in glory; sown in weakness, raised in power; sown a natural body, raised a spiritual body. If there is a natural body, there is also a spiritual body.*"

1 Corinthians 15:42–44 HCSB

With our new bodies, there will be no more sickness and death. *(vv. 42)* "*…it is…raised in incorruption…*"

"incorruption" means *unending existence.*

With our new bodies, there will be no more disgrace because of sin. *(vv. 43a)* *"It is…sown in dishonor, raised in glory…"*

"dishonor" means *disgrace* or *shame*.

"glory" means *dignity* and *honor*.

With our new bodies, there will be no more giving in to temptation. *(vv. 43b)* *"…it is…sown in weakness, raised in power."*

"power" means *miraculous power*. (The English word "dynamite" comes from this word.)

The lust of the flesh, the lust of the eyes, and the pride in one's lifestyle—is not from the Father, but is from the world. And the world with its lust is passing away, but the one who does God's will remains forever.
                                                1 John 2:16-17 HCSB

You won't struggle against the "flesh" any more because of your new supernatural body. God will destroy all wickedness that causes us to take our "eyes" off of Christ.

The **"boastful pride"** of this fallen world will be destroyed forever, and will no longer affect you.

Satan (which means **"tempter"**) and his demons will ultimately be cast into the lake of fire forever, no longer having influence on you.

MEMORY VERSE

*"And the world with its lust
is passing away,
but the one who does God's will
remains forever."*
1 John 2:17 HCSB

THE "WONDER" OF HEAVEN
(CONTINUED)

*The LORD God took the man
and placed him into the garden of Eden
to work it and watch over it.*
Genesis 2:15 HCSB

TODAY'S UNSTOPPABLE TRUTH

Believers will rule and reign with Christ
in His kingdom.

Will we work in heaven?

Working in heaven may sound strange, but the Bible clearly teaches it. Jesus said:

His master said to him, "Well done, good and faithful slave! You were faithful over a few things; I will put you in charge of many things. Share your master's joy!"

Matthew 25:21 HCSB

I don't know exactly what we'll be doing, but the Bible is clear that believers will rule and reign with Christ in His kingdom. God never intended for man to sit around and do nothing:

*The LORD God took the man and placed him into the garden of Eden **to work it** and watch over it.*

Genesis 2:15 HCSB

Will we know everything when we get to heaven?

For now we see in a mirror dimly, but then face to face; now I know in part, but then I will know fully just as I also have been fully known.

1 Corinthians 13:12 NASB

According to this verse, we're obviously going to have an incredible amount of knowledge, but only God is omniscient (*all-knowing*). Even if we don't know *everything*, we'll have all eternity to get every question answered by God Himself!

Will we get bored being there for all eternity? (Come on, you know you've thought it too!)

*…In Your presence is **fullness of joy**; in Your right hand there are **pleasures forever***.

Psalm 16:11 NASB

...No eye has seen, no ear has heard, no mind has conceived what God has prepared for those who love him.

1 Corinthians 2:9 NIV

You'll never see anything in this life that comes close to what you'll see in heaven. *"...No eye has seen..."*

No matter how we describe heaven, it won't come close to the real thing. *"...No ear has heard..."*

Your mind can't conceive what God has prepared for you, if you're truly His. *"...no mind has conceived what God has prepared for those who love him."*

But notice that it said "those who love Him." How do you know if you really love Him? Jesus said in John 14:15, "If you love Me, you will keep My commandments."

Take an honest look at your life and see if it's marked by obedience to God and His Word. Don't be like the man in Luke 16 who was in torment while seeing what he *could* have had!

MORE TRUTH

What joy that the Bible tells us the great comfort that the best is yet to be. Our outlook goes beyond this world.

Corrie ten Boom

The end will be glorious beyond our wildest dreams—for those who put their trust in Him.

Elisabeth Elliot

MEMORY VERSE

…In Your presence is fullness of joy;
In Your right hand
there are pleasures forever.
Psalm 16:11 NASB

HERE AND NOW

For sin will not rule over you,
because you are not under law but under grace.
Romans 6:14 HCSB

TODAY'S UNSTOPPABLE TRUTH

Live your life with the understanding
that God's return is getting closer.

We've been learning how amazing heaven is going to be when we finally see Jesus face to face. So over the next few days we're going to see how God tells us to live our lives *until* the day He comes for us?

Now the end of all things is near; therefore, be clear-headed and disciplined for prayer. Above all, keep your love for one another at full strength, since love covers a multitude of sins. Be hospitable to one another without complaining. Based on the gift they have received, everyone should use it to serve others, as good managers of the varied grace of God. If anyone speaks, his speech should be like the oracles of God; if anyone serves, his service should be from the strength God provides, so that in everything God may be glorified through Jesus Christ. To Him belong the glory and the power forever and ever. Amen. Dear friends, when the fiery ordeal arises among you to test you, don't be surprised by it, as if something unusual were happening to you. Instead, as you share in the sufferings of the Messiah rejoice, so that you may also rejoice with great joy at the revelation of His glory. If you are ridiculed for the name of Christ, you are blessed, because the Spirit of glory and of God rests on you. None of you, however, should suffer as a murderer, a thief, an evildoer, or as a meddler. But if anyone suffers as a Christian, he should not be ashamed, but should glorify God with that name.

1 Peter 4:7–16 HCSB

The term "clear-headed" (vv. 7) has a three-fold meaning:

1) *To have self-control.*

2) *To put a moderate estimate on yourself* (in other words, don't think too low of yourself and don't think too highly of yourself either).

3) *To curb your sinful passions.*

Until Jesus comes back, we *must* use sound judgment! Paul even told us some of the sins we need to show self-control over as we see the day approaching:

The night is almost gone, and the day is near. Therefore let us lay aside the deeds of darkness and put on the armor of light. Let us behave properly as in the day, not in carousing and drunkenness, not in sexual promiscuity and sensuality, not in strife and jealousy. But put on the Lord Jesus Christ, and make no provision for the flesh in regard to its lusts."

Romans 13:12–14 NASB

"carousing" means *letting loose.*

Paul wasn't saying you can't enjoy life. He's talking about an "anything goes" mentality where nothing is off limits. Remember, we just read in our main passage that we should have "self-control and curb our sinful passions."

"sexual promiscuity" means *sexual intercourse* outside of marriage.

"sensuality" means *unbridled lust* and *excess*.

This word carries the meaning of a person who makes *everything* sexual. It's the guy or girl who turns every comment, conversation or joke into something perverted.

"strife" means to constantly *quarrel* or *debate*.

This is a person who thinks they're wise, BUT the wisest man who ever lived said, "*Keeping away from strife is an honor for a man, but any fool will quarrel*" *(Proverbs 20:3).*

Don't be a person who loves strife, and get away from people who do! Remember, Paul called all of these "deeds of darkness."

"jealousy" means *excitement of mind.*

It's when you let your mind get the best of you. We have to keep our thoughts in check, and the only way to do this is to have God's Word hidden in our hearts so we'll know how to respond when jealousy tries to take over.

MORE TRUTH

We, as God's people, are not only to stay far away
from sin and sinners who would entice us,
but we are to be so like our God
that we mourn over sin.

Kay Arthur

It is easier to stay out of temptation
than to get out of it.

Rick Warren

Temptation is not a sin. Even Jesus was tempted.
The Lord Jesus gives you the strength
needed to resist temptation.

Corrie ten Boom

135

MEMORY VERSE

*Now the end of all things is near;
therefore, be clear-headed
and disciplined for prayer.*
1 Peter 4:7 HCSB

COME TOGETHER

"Follow Me," Jesus told them,
"and I will make you into fishers of men!"
Immediately they left their nets and followed Him.
Mark 1:17-18 HCSB

TODAY'S UNSTOPPABLE TRUTH

Until Christ returns, believers should live
their lives in unity with other Christians.

Yesterday we began looking at 1 Peter 4:7-16 to see how we should live until we're taken to heaven. Let's pick up where we left off:

Above all, keep your love for one another at full strength, since love covers a multitude of sins. Be hospitable to one another without complaining.

1 Peter 4:8-9

It's not always easy to love other people (even other believers).

The term **"full strength"** means *to be stretched out.* Keeping unity in the church (and in your youth group) will sometimes "stretch" you to the limit, but Peter said to work at this "above all." Jesus said:

By this all men will know that you are My disciples, if you have love for one another.

John 13:35

Why would anyone want to be a part of your church (or youth group) if the Christians there don't even like each other?

"hospitable" means to *love strangers*.

Peter takes the idea of unity even farther. Not only are we to have unity with other believers, who are already around us, but we're to show love to complete strangers.

This is why it's so important to welcome and invite new students to your church:

Let love of the brethren continue. Do not neglect to show hospitality to strangers, for by this some have entertained angels without knowing it.
Hebrews 13:1-2 NASB

MEMORY VERSE

*Above all, keep your love for one another
at full strength,
since love covers a multitude of sins.*
1 Peter 4:8 HCSB

WHAT ARE YOU GOING TO DO?

Based on the gift they have received, everyone should use it to serve others, as good managers of the varied grace of God. If anyone speaks, his speech should be like the oracles of God; if anyone serves, his service should be from the strength God provides, so that in everything God may be glorified through Jesus Christ. To Him belong the glory and the power forever and ever. Amen.

1 Peter 4:10-11

TODAY'S UNSTOPPABLE TRUTH

Until Christ returns, believers should live their lives in a way that is useful to the Church.

Every believer is gifted by God to support the church. (vv. 10) "Based on the gift they have received, everyone should use it to serve others…"

The word **"serve"** means to *contribute* and *support*.

What are you doing on a consistent basis to support the work of your church? If you're a Christian God has given you a special "gift" and He expects you to be a good steward of that gift until the day He returns:

"Again, it will be like a man going on a journey, who called his servants and entrusted his property to them. To one he gave five talents of money, to another two talents, and to another one talent, each according to his ability. Then he went on his journey. The man who had received the five talents went at once and put his money to work and gained five more. So also, the one with the two talents gained two more. But the man who had received the one talent went off, dug a hole in the ground and hid his master's money. After a long time the master of those servants returned and settled

accounts with them. The man who had received the five talents brought the other five. 'Master,' he said, 'you entrusted me with five talents. See, I have gained five more.' His master replied, 'Well done, good and faithful servant! You have been faithful with a few things; I will put you in charge of many things. Come and share your master's happiness!' The man with the two talents also came. 'Master,' he said, 'you entrusted me with two talents; see, I have gained two more.' His master replied, 'Well done, good and faithful servant! You have been faithful with a few things; I will put you in charge of many things. Come and share your master's happiness!' Then the man who had received the one talent came. 'Master,' he said, 'I knew that you are a hard man, harvesting where you have not sown and gathering where you have not scattered seed. So I was afraid and went out and hid your talent in the ground. See, here is what belongs to you.' His master replied, 'You wicked, lazy servant! So you knew that I harvest where I have not sown and gather where I have not scattered seed? Well then, you should have put my money on deposit with the bankers, so that when I returned I would have received it back with interest. Take the talent from him and give it to the one who has the ten talents. For everyone who has will be given more, and he will have an abundance. Whoever does not have, even what he has will be taken from him. And throw that worthless servant outside, into the darkness, where there will be weeping and gnashing of teeth.'"

Matthew 25:14-30 NIV

Now, back to our main passage:

We have to be totally dependent on God as we use our gift. *(vv. 11a) "…If anyone speaks, his speech should be like the oracles of God; if anyone serves, his service should be from the strength God provides …"*

We serve God for His glory not our own. *(vv. 11b) "…so that in everything God may be glorified through Jesus Christ. To Him belong the glory and the power…"*

MORE TRUTH ABOUT SERVICE

If you want to discover your spiritual gifts,
start obeying God. As you serve Him,
you will find that He has given you the gifts that
are necessary to follow through in obedience.

Anne Graham Lotz

Christianity, in its purest form, is nothing more
than seeing Jesus. Christian service, in its purest
form, is nothing more than imitating him who
we see. To see his Majesty and to imitate him:
that is the sum of Christianity.

Max Lucado

In the very place where God has put us,
whatever its limitations,
whatever kind of work it may be,
we may indeed serve the Lord Christ.

Elisabeth Elliot

MEMORY VERSE

*Based on the gift they have received,
everyone should use it to serve others,
as good managers of the varied grace of God.*
1 Peter 4:10 HCSB

UNASHAMED

You are the light of the world. A city set on a hill
cannot be hidden; nor does anyone light a lamp
and put it under a basket, but on the lampstand,
and it gives light to all who are in the house.
Let your light shine before men in such a way that
they may see your good works, and glorify your
Father who is in heaven.
Matthew 5:14-16 NASB

TODAY'S UNSTOPPABLE TRUTH

Until Christ returns, believers should be willing
to undergo persecution for the Name of Christ.

Earlier in our 30-day journey, we learned from Paul about standing for Christ even when we're persecuted for our faith. Peter gives us even more insight as we move on in the passage we've been looking at over the last few days:

Dear friends, when the fiery ordeal arises among you to test you, don't be surprised by it, as if something unusual were happening to you. Instead, as you share in the sufferings of the Messiah rejoice, so that you may also rejoice with great joy at the revelation of His glory. If you are ridiculed for the name of Christ, you are blessed, because the Spirit of glory and of God rests on you. None of you, however, should suffer as a murderer, a thief, an evildoer, or as a meddler. But if anyone suffers as a Christian, he should not be ashamed, but should glorify God with that name.

1 Peter 4:12-16 HCSB

Every true believer will face persecution in their life. *(vv. 12)* "*...don't be surprised by it, as if something unusual were happening to you.*"

God has a purpose for allowing persecution in your life. *(vv. 12b)* "*…the fiery ordeal arises among you to test you…*"

We should count it a privilege to suffer with Christ. *(vv. 14)* "*If you are ridiculed for the name of Christ, you are blessed, because the Spirit of…God rests on you.*"

Don't confuse suffering for the Name of Christ with sufferings that are caused by your sin. *(vv. 15)* "*None of you, however, should suffer as a murderer, a thief, an evildoer, or as a meddler.*"

Make sure it's not consequences or discipline from God because of sin.

Don't ever be ashamed or discouraged because you suffer for His Name. *(vv. 16)* "*But if anyone suffers as a Christian, he should not be ashamed, but should glorify God with that name.*"

MEMORY VERSE

*If you are ridiculed for the name of Christ,
you are blessed, because the Spirit of…
God rests on you.*

1 Peter 4:14 HCSB

ARE YOU CONVINCED YET?

For I, the Lord your God, hold your right hand and say to you: Do not fear, I will help you.
Isaiah 41:13 HCSB

TODAY'S UNSTOPPABLE TRUTH

If you're going to stand for Christ no matter what happens, then you *have* to trust Him.

Most of the passages we've looked at over the last few days were written down by the Apostle Paul and the Apostle Peter. Both of these guys knew about suffering for the Name of Christ.

Paul was beheaded because of his faith in Christ. Church tradition says Peter was crucified upside down because he refused to stop sharing the truth about Jesus. If you're going to stand for Christ no matter what happens, then you *have* to trust Him like they did. Listen to some of the things they said before they died:

*For this reason I also suffer these things, but I am not ashamed; for I know whom I have believed and I am convinced that He is able to guard what I have entrusted to Him **until that day**.*

2 Timothy 1:12 NASB

So those who suffer according to God's will should, in doing good, entrust themselves to a faithful Creator.

1 Peter 4:19 HCSB

I am sure of this, that He who started a good work in you will carry it on to completion until the day of Christ Jesus.

Philippians 1:6 HCSB

As we wrap up our 30-day journey together, remember the words from James (the half brother of Jesus):

Therefore be patient, brethren, until the coming of the Lord. The farmer waits for the precious produce of the soil, being patient about it, until it gets the early and late rains. You too be patient; strengthen your hearts, for the coming of the Lord is near.

James 5:7-8 NASB

MEMORY VERSE

*So those who suffer according
to God's will should, in doing good,
entrust themselves to a faithful Creator.*
1 Peter 4:19 HCSB

*My word that comes from My mouth
will not return to Me empty,
but it will accomplish what
I please, and will prosper in what
I send it [to do].*
Isaiah 55:11 HCSB

INDEX OF
MEMORY VERSES

DAY 1

*Blessed be the God and Father of our Lord
Jesus Christ, the Father of mercies
and the God of all comfort.
He comforts us in all our affliction…*
2 Corinthians 1:3–4a HCSB

DAY 2

*Everyone should look out not only
for his own interests,
but also for the interests of others.*
Philippians 2:4 HCSB

DAY 3

So we must not get tired of doing good,
for we will reap at the proper time
if we don't give up.
Galatians 6:9 HCSB

DAY 4

Should we accept only good from God
and not adversity?
Job 2:10b HCSB

DAY 5

I will praise the LORD at all times;
His praise will always be on my lips.
Psalm 34:1 HCSB

DAY 6

For our proud confidence is this:
the testimony of our conscience,
that in holiness and godly sincerity...
we have conducted ourselves
in the world...
2 Corinthians 1:12 NASB

DAY 7

Many adversities come to the one
who is righteous, but the LORD
delivers him from them all.
Psalm 34:19 HCSB

DAY 8

My word…will not return to Me empty,
without accomplishing what I desire,
and without succeeding in the matter
for which I sent it.
Isaiah 55:11 NASB

DAY 9

…you welcomed it not as a human message,
but as it truly is the message of God, which
also works effectively in you believers.
1 Thessalonians 2:13 HCSB

DAY 10

*For I assure you: Until heaven and earth
pass away, not the smallest letter or
one stroke of a letter will pass from the law
until all things are accomplished.*
Matthew 5:18 HCSB

DAY 11

*For My thoughts are not your thoughts,
nor are your ways My ways,
declares the LORD. For as the heavens
are higher than the earth, so are My ways
higher than your ways and
My thoughts than your thoughts.*
Isaiah 55:8 HCSB

DAY 12

*In fact, all those who want to live
a godly life in Christ Jesus
will be persecuted.*
2 Timothy 3:12 HCSB

DAY 13

*Do not repay anyone evil for evil.
Be careful to do what is right
in the eyes of everybody.*
Romans 12:17 NIV

DAY 14

*Do not be conquered by evil,
but conquer evil with good.*
Romans 12:21 HCSB

DAY 15

*This is the verdict: Light has come
into the world, but men loved darkness
instead of light because their deeds were evil.*
John 3:19 NIV

DAY 16

*But if, in fact, our gospel is veiled,
it is veiled to those who are perishing.*
2 Corinthians 4:3 HCSB

DAY 17

*…it is appointed for men to die once and
after this comes judgment.*
Hebrews 9:27 NASB

DAY 18

*Knowing their works and their thoughts,
I have come to gather all nations and
languages; they will come and see My glory.*
Isaiah 66:18 HCSB

DAY 19

*A good man produces good things from his
storeroom of good, and an evil man produces
evil things from his storeroom of evil.*
Matthew 12:35 HCSB

DAY 20

Nothing in all creation is hidden
from God's sight. Everything is uncovered
and laid bare before the eyes of him
to whom we must give account.
Hebrews 4:13 NIV

DAY 21

Precious in the sight of the LORD
is the death of his saints.
Psalm 116:15 NIV

DAY 22

…No eye has seen, no ear has heard,
no mind has conceived what
God has prepared for those who love him.
1 Corinthians 2:9 NIV

DAY 23

Praise Him, all His angels;
praise Him, all His hosts…
Let them praise the name of the L<small>ORD</small>,
for He commanded, and they were created.
Psalm 148:2, 5 HCSB

DAY 24

*"nd the world with its lust is passing away,
but the one who does
God's will remains forever.*

1 John 2:17 HCSB

DAY 25

*…In Your presence is fullness of joy;
In Your right hand
there are pleasures forever.*

Psalm 16:11 NASB

DAY 26

Now the end of all things is near;
therefore, be clear-headed
and disciplined for prayer.
1 Peter 4:7 HCSB

DAY 27

Above all, keep your love
for one another at full strength,
since love covers a multitude of sins.
1 Peter 4:8 HCSB

DAY 28

*Based on the gift they have received,
everyone should use it to serve others,
as good managers of the varied grace of God.*
1 Peter 4:10 HCSB

DAY 29

*If you are ridiculed for the name of Christ,
you are blessed, because the Spirit of...
God rests on you.*
1 Peter 4:14 HCSB

DAY 30

*So those who suffer according to God's will
should, in doing good,
entrust themselves to a faithful Creator.*
1 Peter 4:19 HCSB

NOTES

Your thoughts and notes from this devotional
about God's unstoppable plan for *your* life!

UNSTOPPABLE for girls